Haunted Houses

by Dinah Williams

Consultant: Troy Taylor
President of the American Ghost Society

BEARPORT
PUBLISHING

New York, New York

Credits

Cover and Title Page, © Shaun Lowe/istockphoto.com, Tyler Stalman/istockphoto.com, and Kevin Russ/istockphoto.com; 4–5, © Naude/Shutterstock; 6, Courtesy of Martha and Darwin Linn/Villisca Axe Murder House and the Olson-Linn Museum; 7L, Courtesy of Martha and Darwin Linn/Villisca Axe Murder House and the Olson-Linn Museum; 7R, © Shutterstock; 8, © AP Photo/HO; 9L, © Winchester Mystery House, San Jose, CA.; 9R, © James Leynse/CORBIS; 10, © Natalie Smothers/DreamChild MindWorks 2007; 11TL, © ajt/Shutterstock; 11TR, Courtesy of The Fall River Historical Society; 11BL, Courtesy of The Fall River Historical Society; 11BR, Courtesy of The Fall River Historical Society; 12, Photo by Robert Thivierge; 13T, © Andresr/Shutterstock; 13B, Courtesy of Library of Congress Prints and Photographs Division; 14, © Shutterstock; 15L, © Snark/Art Resource, NY; 15R, Courtesy of Library of Congress Prints and Photographs Division; 16, © Bettmann/CORBIS; 17, © Perennou Nuridsany/Photo Researchers, Inc.; 18, © Amanda Baird/BlackDoll Photography; 19L, Courtesy of Library of Congress Prints and Photographs Division; 19R, © Amanda Dague; 20, © John & Kim Hirchak/Ghost Walk of Old Wilmington; 21T, © CVP/Shutterstock; 21B, © Getty Images/The Bridgeman Art Library; 22, © Adam Thrasher; 23L, © Richard T. Nowitz/CORBIS; 23R, © Photo illustration courtesy Galveston Historical Foundation/David Canright; 24, © 13th Door Haunted House 2003, photo by Raymond Latocki; 25T, © Sebastian Kaulitzki/Shutterstock; 25B, © plastique/Shutterstock; 26, © M. Timothy O'Keefe/Alamy; 27T, © image100/SuperStock; 27B, © Damian White/Photo: www.flickr.com/photos/damian_white; 31, © Elixirpix/Shutterstock.com.

Publisher: Kenn Goin
Editorial Director: Adam Siegel
Creative Director: Spencer Brinker
Design: Dawn Beard Creative
Photo Researcher: Beaura Kathy Ringrose

Library of Congress Cataloging-in-Publication Data

Williams, Dinah.
 Haunted houses / by Dinah Williams.
    p. cm. — (Scary places)
 Includes bibliographical references and index.
 ISBN-13: 978-1-59716-573-0 (library binding)
 ISBN-10: 1-59716-573-5 (library binding)
 1. Haunted houses—Juvenile literature. I. Title.

 BF1475.W55 2008
 133.1'22—dc22

                                2007040424

For more information, write to Bearport Publishing Company, Inc., 45 West 21st Street, Suite 3B, New York, New York, 10010. Printed in the United States of America.

20 19 18 17 16 15 14 13 12 11

Contents

Haunted Houses

There is something frightening about a creaky, old house. Anything might have happened under its roof. A family could have been murdered there. A young woman might have died from a sudden illness. Perhaps an old man slipped on the stairs and broke his neck. The ghosts of such people might still be in some houses, trying to tell their stories—and haunting the living.

Why do ghosts haunt houses? According to some, they are the **spirits** of people who died so suddenly they don't know they're dead. Other ghosts stick around to seek **revenge** on their killers. Yet others may have lived in the house so long they forgot they're supposed to leave. In the 11 haunted houses in this book, you'll meet the ghost of a troubled president, a Texas princess, a pig named Jodie, and a playful **poltergeist** named George.

The 2:00 A.M. Train

Villisca Axe Murder House, Villisca, Iowa

What is a ghost? Many people believe it is the spirit of a person who has stayed on Earth after death. Ghost hunters are people who try to find these mysterious spirits. They usually aren't scared of the ghostly activity they discover. Yet who wouldn't be frightened to relive a brutal murder?

Villisca Axe
Murder House

In the early-morning hours of June 10, 1912, a stranger entered the Moore family home. He snuck quietly from room to room. By the time he left, eight people had been killed with an ax. The police didn't have enough **evidence** to charge anyone with the crime. The killer was never caught. Yet some believe his spirit still haunts the house.

Ghost hunters who have spent the night at the Moore house often notice a ghostly fog. It moves from room to room, just like the killer did the night of his crime. It is followed by the awful sound of dripping blood.

These spooky events usually happen at 2:00 A.M. This is the time when a train passes through the town of Villisca. Some believe that the murderer used the noise from the speeding locomotive to mask the sound of his bloody acts. Perhaps the creepy sights and sounds in the middle of the night are actually the killer's ghost reliving his murders almost 100 years later.

The murder of the Moore family made headlines.

In 1930, Homer and Bonnie Ritter rented the house in Villisca. Night after night, Bonnie woke to the strange sight of a man with an ax at the foot of her bed. Homer then began hearing the sound of someone walking up and down the stairs in the middle of the night. The Ritters moved out shortly thereafter.

Building a Home for Ghosts

Winchester Mystery House, San Jose, California

Few things are scarier than being chased by an angry ghost. Unless, of course, it is being chased by a huge crowd of ghosts. Sarah Winchester would know. She spent almost half her life trying to outrun thousands of angry spirits.

Winchester Mystery House

Sarah Winchester believed in ghosts. After her husband, William, died in 1881, she was sad and wanted to talk to him one last time. So Sarah hired a **medium** to contact his ghost. What she learned would forever change her life.

Through the medium, William told Sarah that the millions of dollars he had left her were **cursed**. The money had been earned by selling deadly Winchester rifles. Sarah had to build a house for the spirits of the thousands of people killed by the guns. As long as she kept building, the ghosts would not kill her.

What could Sarah do? She bought a six-room house in 1884 and began building. Thirty-eight years later, the maze-like house had 160 rooms. Even though workmen built around the clock, death finally found Sarah. She died at age 83 in 1922. Today, visitors to the house can find Sarah, too—her ghost has been seen wandering its many hallways.

A Winchester rifle

Sarah found comfort in the number 13, which she considered lucky. In the Winchester Mystery House there are 13 bathrooms, 13 windows in some rooms, 13 palm trees lining the main driveway, and 13 stairs on most of the staircases.

Sarah Winchester

The Bloody End to the Bordens

Lizzie Borden House, Fall River, Massachusetts

People who die in violent and unexpected ways are thought to be more likely to return as ghosts. Perhaps they are seeking revenge for their murders. Or maybe they don't know they are dead. Few died as suddenly and violently as Abby and Andrew Borden, so it's no wonder they are still at home.

Lizzie Borden House

On the hot morning of August 4, 1892, Abby Borden was making a bed in the guest room of her home. Someone came up behind her and crushed her head with 19 blows from an ax. About 90 minutes later, her husband, Andrew, was killed in the same way. Some people thought that their daughter, Lizzie, committed the crime. However, there was not enough evidence to prove it.

Lizzie Borden

Today, the Borden house is an **inn** where people can spend the night. Yet guests should beware. Some visitors say they have heard the voice of a woman quietly crying. Others have reported seeing an older woman dressed in clothes from the 1890s cleaning the guest room. They have even been awakened in the middle of the night to see this same woman tucking them into bed. Maybe it is the ghost of Abby, still thinking she is tucking in her darling Lizzie.

Lizzie's parents after the murder

Using photos from the Borden crime scene, the owners of the inn have recreated the way the rooms looked on the day that Lizzie's parents were killed. They also serve a breakfast similar to the one that the Bordens ate the morning they died.

Death at the Deane

The Deane House, Calgary, Alberta, Canada

A boardinghouse is a building where people rent rooms for short periods of time. With so many guests, a boardinghouse is bound to have a rich history. The Deane House is no exception. C. L. Jacques began renting rooms to people there in 1929. According to some, a few of his guests have never left.

The Deane House

One of the many staff members who saw the Deane House ghosts was Alez Jackci. He was working late one night when a man floated down the hallway. The bottoms of his legs were missing. The ghost went down the stairs and out the door. Others have heard loud footsteps on the top floor. According to **legend**, there is a bloodstain in the attic that will not go away—even after it has been cleaned.

Why are there so many ghosts at the Deane House? When it was a boardinghouse, a number of unusual deaths took place there. A young woman jumped from the second-story window. A man was shot on the porch. In 1952, a husband stabbed his wife to death. He then killed himself. Perhaps the spirits of these victims are not ready to leave yet. One thing is certain, however. With so many ghosts, the Deane House is one of Canada's most haunted places.

A Native American ghost has often been spotted at the Deane House. Some say this is because the house was built on an Indian **burial ground**. One woman who went into the basement was greeted by the spirit. He told her that the site was **sacred** and she shouldn't be there. He then disappeared.

Lincoln Can't Leave

The White House, Washington, D.C.

Many ghosts are said to haunt the White House. The ghost of President Andrew Jackson has been spotted there, as well as Dolley Madison, the wife of President James Madison. The most famous ghostly visitor, however, is Abraham Lincoln.

The White House

One morning in the spring of 1865, Abraham Lincoln woke from a terrible dream. In it, he saw a **corpse** in the White House guarded by soldiers. When he asked who was dead, a soldier replied, "The President was killed by an **assassin**." Less than a month later, on April 14, 1865, Lincoln was shot to death by John Wilkes Booth.

Since his death, Lincoln's ghost has been seen a number of times at the White House. In the 1940s, Queen Wilhelmina of the Netherlands saw him when she was visiting President Franklin D. Roosevelt. She was awakened by a knock on her door. When she opened it, there stood the ghost of Abraham Lincoln. She immediately fainted. When she awoke, he was gone.

President Abraham Lincoln

Lincoln's son, William, died in the White House from typhoid fever in 1862. He was only 11 years old. His mother, Mary Todd Lincoln, claimed his ghost visited her every night.

Mary Todd Lincoln

The House of Horror

Amityville House, Amityville, New York

A poltergeist is a spirit that makes itself known in a home by making loud noises and moving objects. In some cases, it can also hurt people. *Poltergeists*, however, seems like a tame word for the angry spirits that may have terrorized a house in Amityville, New York.

The house in Amityville

On the night of November 14, 1974, 23-year-old Ronald DeFeo, Jr., took out his rifle and shot his father. Within the next 15 minutes, he would murder all six members of his family. The brutal crime made headlines in many newspapers. Unfortunately, this was not the last time people would hear about shocking events taking place in this house.

One year later, the Lutz family moved in. In the 28 days they lived there, they claimed the house began to change. Flies started swarming around the windows. Slime oozed from the walls. Toilet bowls began to turn black.

The Lutzes' daughter developed a disturbing imaginary friend. It was a pig named Jodie, that seemed very real. Her parents saw its glowing red eyes, heard it squeal, and even saw the animal's hoofprints in the snow. Other creepy events also took place in the house. Mrs. Lutz claimed that invisible hands grabbed her. Unable to stand the haunting any longer, the family fled one night, never to return.

Many people who have investigated the Amityville haunting believe that most of the terrifying events described by the Lutzes never happened. Yet that hasn't stopped thousands of people from being fascinated by the house's famous and spooky past.

The Problem with Poison

The Myrtles Plantation, St. Francisville, Louisiana

The Myrtles **Plantation** is considered one of America's most haunted houses. Many of the ghostly tales about the home may be more **fiction** than fact, but that doesn't stop the stories from being told—and even being believed.

The Myrtles Plantation

Clarke Woodruff ran the Myrtles Plantation in the early 1800s. According to legend, he was not always kind to the people who worked for him. One time he caught his slave Chloe **eavesdropping** on one of his conversations. He was so angry that he had one of her ears cut off.

Rather than get upset, Chloe wanted to find a way to show that she still cared about the Woodruff family. So Chloe baked them a cake containing a small amount of poisonous flowers. Once they ate it, she imagined she would kindly nurse the sick family back to health. The poison, however, was too strong. Mrs. Woodruff and her two daughters died. When people found out what she did, Chloe was hanged.

Since then, people have claimed that Chloe's ghost haunts the Myrtles. A past owner even accidentally took a photo of her. In it, Chloe appears in the **turban** she wore to cover her missing ear.

The haunted mirror at the Myrtles

According to some people, the spirits of Mrs. Woodruff and her daughters are trapped in a large mirror at the Myrtles. Photographs of it show ghostly handprints inside the mirror's glass. Even after the glass was replaced, the ghostly handprints returned.

19

Hanging Around the House

Price-Gause House, Wilmington, North Carolina

The dead do not like to be disturbed. One sure way to stir up ghosts is to build on the land where their bodies are buried. No wonder the Price-Gause House on **Gallows** Hill has had more than its share of poltergeists. It sits on top of a burial ground for criminals.

The Price-Gause House

Gallows Hill in Wilmington, North Carolina, was the site of many hangings. The bodies of criminals were often buried right there if no one claimed them. As the town of Wilmington grew, the gallows were eventually taken down. Houses were built on top of the land where the dead bodies rested.

A gallows

Dr. William Price built the Price-Gause House on Gallows Hill in 1843. After his family moved in, they realized they were not alone. In hot summer weather, the upstairs window became covered in frost. The word *Help* was often seen written on the icy glass.

Even today, footsteps are still heard going up and down the stairs. Doors mysteriously open and close. Current residents have named one of the playful ghosts George. How do they know when he is around? Sometimes a chair begins to rock back and forth by itself. At other times this playful poltergeist pulls a quilt from a bed while someone is still sleeping in it.

Salem, Massachusetts, is home to another famous Gallows Hill. People accused of witchcraft were hanged there during the Salem Witch Trials in 1692. Like the hill in Wilmington, it is also haunted. Mary Easty was hanged in Salem in September 1692 for being a witch. Shortly thereafter, her ghost was said to have returned to declare her innocence.

These women were accused of being witches and were hanged.

A Glamorous Ghost

Ashton Villa Mansion, Galveston, Texas

Many people believe that when a person's spirit returns as a ghost, it appears as the person did at the time of his or her death. The spirit is often even wearing the same clothes. That's good news for Bettie Ashton Brown. She was always dressed like a princess—so she looks great as a ghost.

Ashton Villa Mansion

Beautiful Bettie Ashton Brown was born into a wealthy family in 1855. She spent her **pampered** life at Ashton Villa, buying fancy fans and dresses. She had many boyfriends but never married. Some claim Bettie loved the expensive items she collected more than any man.

After Bettie died in 1920, her beloved **mansion** was turned into a museum. Her ghost is said to still visit often. A museum worker once came across her arguing with a dark-haired ghost at the piano. He overheard the ghost saying to Bettie, "It is foolish for any man to talk to you about marriage. You couldn't really love anyone." The dark-haired man then disappeared, leaving behind a sobbing Bettie.

Visitors to the museum have been surprised to hear the ghostly sound of piano playing. Perhaps it is Bettie, trying to heal a broken heart.

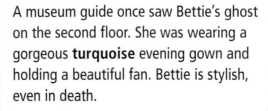

A museum guide once saw Bettie's ghost on the second floor. She was wearing a gorgeous **turquoise** evening gown and holding a beautiful fan. Bettie is stylish, even in death.

Thrills at a Theater

The 13th Door Haunted House, Tigard, Oregon

Every Halloween, spooky haunted houses open to scare their customers. Often, people are hired to pretend to be frightening creatures during the holiday. Yet the 13th Door Haunted House has ghosts all year-round—and not the kind that get paid.

The 13th Door Haunted House

Built in the 1970s, a movie theater called the Regal Cinema has a dark and haunted past. Some claim the spirit of a man who killed himself in the storage room has never left. His ghost is said to have pushed employees down the stairs. Workers also reported seeing film reels mysteriously flying off the projectors. Muddy handprints were found on the film screens.

After the theater closed, it was turned into the 13th Door—a spooky haunted house for Halloween. Since then, more ghosts have been seen there, including a girl in an old-fashioned dress and a man dressed in black who is called Lurch.

The owner said he doesn't mind "the cold breezes, the tapping, touching, footsteps, voices, or dark shadows" caused by the ghosts. His employees, however, don't always agree. Many have threatened to quit after working one night there.

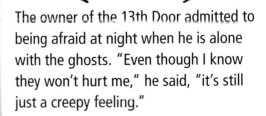

The owner of the 13th Door admitted to being afraid at night when he is alone with the ghosts. "Even though I know they won't hurt me," he said, "it's still just a creepy feeling."

The White Witch

Rose Hall Great House, Montego Bay, Jamaica

In the early 1800s, Annie Palmer married the owner of Rose Hall—a beautiful mansion. The young woman was lucky to live in such a gorgeous home. Unfortunately, those who lived with Annie were not. They would soon know why this cruel woman was called the White Witch of Rose Hall.

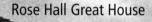
Rose Hall Great House

Although she was a small woman, Annie was powerful. She is thought to have murdered all three of her husbands. She had the slaves on her sugar plantation beaten and tortured for her amusement. Annie even built a **dungeon** 16 feet (5 m) deep in the middle of her house. She imprisoned slaves there who tried to run away. Many of them ended up dying there, too.

In 1831, Annie became interested in a handsome young man. Unfortunately, he liked her housekeeper, Millicent. So Annie cast a **spell** on her. Millicent died nine days later. The housekeeper's grandfather was so angry that he strangled Annie to death.

Annie's body was buried in a cement coffin. Yet her spirit remains at Rose Hall. When a family tried to live there in 1905, Annie's ghost supposedly pushed a maid off the balcony to her death. The family fled and the beautiful home remained empty until 1965—when it was turned into a museum.

The coffin of the White Witch

Even though Rose Hall is now a museum, the White Witch is still scaring people more than 175 years after her death. Annie's ghost is said to slam doors and windows, turn water on and off, and even appear to some visitors.

The Deane House
Calgary, Alberta, Canada

A former boardinghouse full of ghosts

Villisca Axe Murder House
Villisca, Iowa

A ghostly fog follows the path of a murderer

Lizzie Borden House
Fall River, Massachusetts

An ax murderer cuts two lives short

The 13th Door Haunted House
Tigard, Oregon

A real Halloween haunted house

Amityville House
Amityville, New York

A house so haunted it forced its owners to leave

Winchester Mystery House
San Jose, California

A home for ghosts built by a worried widow

Ashton Villa Mansion
Galveston, Texas

A Texas princess still dresses to impress

The Myrtles Plantation
St. Francisville, Louisiana

The ghost of a slave who did not mean to commit murder

Rose Hall Great House
Montego Bay, Jamaica

Home of the White Witch

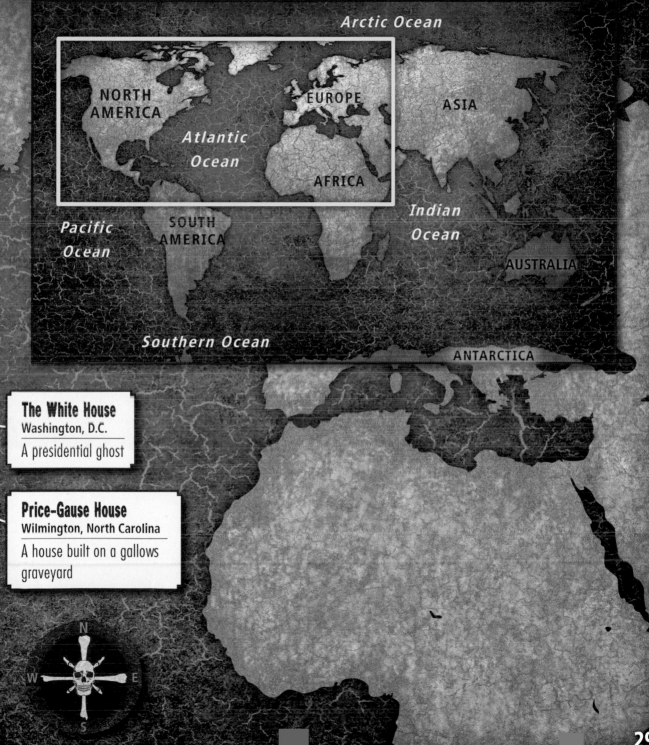

Arctic Ocean

NORTH AMERICA

EUROPE

ASIA

Atlantic Ocean

AFRICA

Indian Ocean

Pacific Ocean

SOUTH AMERICA

AUSTRALIA

Southern Ocean

ANTARCTICA

The White House
Washington, D.C.

A presidential ghost

Price-Gause House
Wilmington, North Carolina

A house built on a gallows graveyard

Glossary

assassin (uh-SASS-in) a person who kills a politically important person

burial ground (BER-ee-uhl GROUND) land where dead bodies are buried

corpse (KORPS) a dead body

cursed (KURST) bringing unhappiness or bad luck

dungeon (DUHN-juhn) a dark prison cell, usually underground

eavesdropping (EEVZ-*drop*-ing) secretly listening to another person's conversation

evidence (EV-uh-duhnss) objects or information that can be used to prove whether something is true

fiction (FIK-shuhn) a story that has characters and events that are made up

gallows (GAL-ohz) a wooden frame used to hang criminals

inn (IN) a small hotel

legend (LEJ-uhnd) a story handed down from long ago that is often based on some facts but cannot be proven true

mansion (MAN-shuhn) a large and grand house

medium (MEE-dee-uhm) a person through whom others seek to communicate with the spirits of the dead

pampered (PAM-purd) treated with too much care and attention

plantation (plan-TAY-shuhn) a large farm where crops, such as cotton, coffee, or tea, are grown

poltergeist (POHL-tur-gyest) a ghost that makes itself known in a home by making loud noises and moving objects

revenge (ri-VENJ) punishment for something that has been unfairly done

sacred (SAY-krid) holy

spell (SPEL) words that are supposed to have magical powers

spirits (SPIHR-its) supernatural creatures, such as ghosts

turban (TUR-buhn) a covering for one's head, often made by wrapping a long scarf or piece of cloth around the head

turquoise (TUR-koiz) a blue-green color

Bibliography

Belanger, Jeff. *The World's Most Haunted Places: From the Secret Files of Ghostvillage.com.* Franklin Lakes, NJ: New Page Books (2004).

Belanger, Jeff, ed. *Encyclopedia of Haunted Places: Ghostly Locales from Around the World.* Franklin Lakes, NJ: New Page Books (2005).

Holzer, Hans. *Hans Holzer's Haunted America.* New York: Barnes & Noble (1993).

Taylor, Troy. *The Haunting of America: Ghosts & Legends of America's Haunted Past.* Alton, IL: Whitechapel Productions Press (2001).

Read More

Guy, John A. *Ghosts: Haunted Houses & Spooky Stories.* Hauppauge, NY: Barron's Educational Series (1999).

Krohn, Katherine. *Haunted Houses.* Mankato, MN: Edge Books (2006).

Oxlade, Chris. *The Mystery of Haunted Houses.* Chicago: Heinemann Library (2006).

Learn More Online

To learn more about haunted houses, visit
www.bearportpublishing.com/ScaryPlaces

Index

About the Author

Dinah Williams is a nonfiction editor and writer who has produced dozens of books for children. She lives in New Jersey.